Two-Home Families:
A Family System's Approach
to Divorce Therapy

Two-Home Families:
A Family System's Approach to Divorce Therapy

A Step-By-Step Model for Preserving Parent-Child Relationships After Divorce Strikes

For Mental Health Professionals, Mediators, and Attorneys who work with divorcing couples and their children.

Brenda Dozier, Ph.D., LMFT, LPC

iUniverse, Inc.
New York Lincoln Shanghai

Two-Home Families:
A Family System's Approach to Divorce Therapy
A Step-By-Step Model for Preserving Parent-Child Relationships After Divorce Strikes

iUniverse, Inc.

For information address:
iUniverse, Inc.
2021 Pine Lake Road, Suite 100
Lincoln, NE 68512
www.iuniverse.com

Information in this book is not intended to replace the services of an attorney, mediator, or qualified mental health professional. This model is based on clinical data; and there are no empirical claims made by the author.

Names and identifying characteristics of individuals in this book have been changed to protect confidentiality.

ISBN: 0-595-31725-1

Printed in the United States of America

This book is dedicated to my lovely daughter, Lori Renee Hinkle, who has been a constant reminder that there are rewards when parents *act right* after divorce. Without a doubt, the most joyful day in my life was the day Lori was born. She had to make many sacrifices while I was in graduate school, and she was always forgiving of my shortcomings and proud of my accomplishments. It has been so delightful to see her grow into the fine woman she is today, and I look forward to watching her as she continues to savor the gifts of life. Thank you, Lori. *I love you. God Loves You.*

Acknowledgment

I must acknowledge all the families who have offered themselves as gifts to me. They opened up very sacred places in their hearts and souls and so willingly shared their hopes, fears, and dreams. Adults and children in my office taught me the struggles of building two homes when many times it would have been easier to throw in the towel. The years and tears I spent with these families made it possible for me to write this book.

Contents

Introduction

The primary goal of this book is to provide mental health professionals the tools needed to help families preserve post-divorce relationships between all family members. Another mission of this book is to help the counselor facilitate the legal system in insuring that parent-child relationships continue for mothers and fathers after divorce unless one or both adults have violated their rights to their children. <u>This model is not intended for use in situations where one or both of the parents are a danger to the children or a parent is a threat to the other parent!</u>

To apply my Two-Home Family model, it is imperative to use a Family Systems theoretical approach with children and adults from divorced families. The information in this book will help insure that you do just that.

Keep in mind that this approach does not undermine the need for individual counseling with one of the adults or with children who are suffering the consequences of divorce. Grief issues will abound all members of the post-divorce family. But, once you begin a therapist-client relationship that targets individual counseling, you may not be able to reverse the process and serve as the Two-Home Family therapist. You may not even realize that you have already developed an alliance with one party. I strongly recommend that you provide one service—individual counseling or Two-Home Family Therapy—not both. When you have been the individual counselor for one parent or the children, refer the family to another therapist for the Two-Home Family work.

Likewise, many couples reap benefits from hiring a divorce mediator to help them settle their economic disputes. Find a trained mediator in your community to refer couples. Both parties also have to hire separate attorneys to represent them in their divorce. The attorneys will process the work done in mediation and/or the Two-Home Family work and convert it into the needed format for the legal decree.

Be bold and good luck as you work with one of the most challenging client populations in the mental health field!

Marketing Yourself as a Divorce Expert

This book will provide the tools necessary for you to identify and market yourself as a divorce expert in your community. The first step in developing an effective marketing plan is gaining credibility as a divorce expert. Of course, in order to identify yourself as an expert on divorce you must do some initial homework:

1. Know the divorce rate in your community (obtain this from the court system). Compare this to the national average.

2. Know what programs divorcing adults are mandated to participate in by your courts and all other resources that are available (collaborative law, divorce support groups for adults and children, church singles ministry, etc.).

3. Obtain data about your state's divorce legislation (e.g., geographical relocation by either parent; child support guidelines; grandparent rights).

4. Find out who the top divorce attorneys are in your area.

5. Design a simple brochure that advertises you as a Two-Home Family divorce expert. Give a brief overview of how your approach preserves parent-child relationships. A sample brochure is in the Appendices.

6. Contact the American BAR Association and volunteer to speak at an upcoming meeting. Likewise, volunteer to lead conferences, seminars, talks, etc. with your local church singles ministry, agencies servicing families, civic groups, hospitals, and at schools. Always keep your talk limited to one subject area in your Two-Home Family model. You can always go back again and offer another topic at a future meeting.

7. Meet the top divorce attorneys and leave your brochure. Next, introduce yourself to all other attorneys in your community and leave your brochure with them.

8. Meet the Family Court/Circuit Court Judges (and make sure you meet their secretaries and assistants) and leave your brochure with them.

9. Meet physicians (pediatricians, OB-GYNs, general/family practitioners, etc.) and distribute your brochure.

10. Introduce yourself to ministers (don't forget youth ministers and singles ministry directors) in your local churches and let them know how you help divorcing family members.

11. Contact primary, secondary, and higher education officials and let them know who you are (and, leave your brochure).

12. Run an ad in your local newspaper's business section about your expertise. Focus on one major aspect of services you provide under your Two-Home Family model.

13. Contact other mental health professionals in your community and let them know about your specialty in the divorce area.

Contracting Two-Home Family Divorce Therapy

To stay on track and maintain effectiveness, several components of the Two-Home Family model need to be included when you initially contract with the divorcing parents: an overview of the Two-Home model, number of sessions and participants in each session, release of information, and time allotted to discuss sensitive issues. I will expand on each of these in this section.

Two-Home Family Model of Therapy

When one parent contacts you and wants to secure therapy services for either him/her and/or the children, make sure you meet with the adult before you interview the children. The best-case scenario is to get both parents in the first session. In some cases, one of the parents will want you to meet with the children in an attempt to get you to form an alliance with him/her and the children against the other parent. By meeting with the adults first, you will not put the children in the position of reporting to therapy to disclose negative/false information about the other parent. Some adults are so hurt and angry about the dissolution of a marriage that they sacrifice their children by coaching or brainwashing them with toxic information about the other parent. A child-centered approach to divorce will protect children from some of this trauma.

Before you begin therapy, it is critical for you to determine whether or not a legal battle is in process. Your intake form should generate information about the involvement of attorneys (see Appendices for a sample).

When you do meet with one of the adults alone, let him/her know that you will also need to meet with the other parent before you meet the children. Use an intake form as a safety-screening tool (sample intake is in the Appendices). When there is no threat of harm, this is the time to find out if the parent will be willing to meet jointly with the other parent. If the client in your office tries to convince you that the other parent will not participate, ask for a phone number and contact the other parent while the client is still with you. If you do not get a contact number, inform the client with you that you will go through his/her attorney to contact the other parent (as you will see in the next section of this book, you will have a release authorizing you to do so). When you speak with the attorney, ask him/her to contact the other parent's attorney and request that his/her client contact you. If that is unsuccessful, ask your client/parent's attorney to file a motion that would mandate all family members to participate in therapy with you.

You have to explain that if you meet with the adults in separate sessions, therapy will be longer in duration, and as a consequence, more costly than when they can meet together. Because divorcing couples are already so concerned about finances, this may facilitate their willingness to meet together with you. It is also beneficial to let both parents know that if a session begins to emotionally escalate, you may use part of their time to meet with each of them separately. Again, this is less costly and more efficient than scheduling appointments with each parent on two different days of the week.

Have a carefully planned out introduction of your Two-Home Family model that you will use with the parents at the beginning of the first session. You must provide the structure early in treatment and maintain control throughout the process in order to be effective. It is also important that you sell your approach to both parents. The best way to make that sell is by telling them that you want to help them help their children experience as little trauma as possible following divorce. Most parents want what is best for their children. This is the time for you to challenge and confront the parents if they resist working from a Two-Home therapy model. Generate questions that will jolt the parents into recognizing that if they do not co-parent, they may possibly be sabotaging their own future relationship with their children. In other words, parents have the opportunity to build-up relationships with their children or tear them down. The divorce ground is fertile to grow either lifelong parent-child relations that are close and positive in nature or distant and bitter. This process begins long before children leave home as late teens and young adults.

This is a difficult time for the parents because they are required to grieve the loss of the marriage and simultaneously develop an effective co-parental relationship. To separate the former spousal role from the parental role can seem impossible. When the adults find a good support system this task will become easier to accomplish. Make sure you offer referrals for divorce support groups immediately. Basically, you have the opportunity to show the adults how their behaviors after divorce will either contribute to future positive parent-child relations or increase negative interactions. And, it is time to commend parents when they are willing to work together. By being as cordial as possible with the other parent, they are making an investment in their future relationship with their children, and they are minimizing child maladjustment to divorce.

Number of Sessions and Participants in Each Session

Initialize an eight-week contract and have both adults sign a simple agreement to participate in eight sessions. A sample of this agreement is in the Appendices. During the eight sessions when a Cooperative Co-Parenting plan is developed, the first three are reserved for meeting with both parents together, children are seen in the fourth session, one parent and children in the fifth, the other parent and children in the sixth, any other significant adults in the seventh (new spouses, live-in adults, grandparents), and the final session is conducted with all members of both homes. The number of sessions will be greater in cases of developing a Parallel Co-Parenting plan. It may take up to 20 sessions; 12 will serve as a minimum. In this situation, both parents will be seen separately, the children and parent-child sessions will be the same as in the Cooperative model, sessions with significant others will also require two separate sessions, and the final session will be conducted with members in each home in separate sessions.

Release of Information

Obtain the written approval of both parents to speak to any significant others in the post-divorce family's life. It is important to have the freedom to speak with the attorneys, grandparents, new spouses/new significant others, teachers, church staff, etc. A sample copy of this comprehensive release form is in the Appendices.

Time Allotted to Discuss Sensitive Issues

There will be times when one parent is willing to talk about a particular problem that is sensitive in nature, and the other vehemently refuses. It is often helpful to negotiate with the parents and ask them to discuss a topic for ten minutes at a time. At the end of that time, it is important for you to stop the transaction and compliment them for following through with that commitment. Then help them summarize any resolution they arrived at or facilitate an agreement to reevaluate the issue in a future session. In some cases, they may contract for ten more minutes; particularly if they were close to resolution.

Structuring the Sessions

As mentioned earlier, the number of sessions needed to complete the Two-Home Family model will depend on whether a Cooperative Co-parenting plan or a Parallel Co-parenting plan is appropriate. In an effort to maintain clarity, the following sections will assume a Cooperative Co-Parenting plan is being developed.

The 90-minute Hour:

Allow 90 minutes for your Two-Home Family sessions. This gives you the much-needed maneuverability and some down time in-between sessions.

Beginning, In-Between, and Ending

Beginning: Getting the Parents In

Have both parties complete the intake form prior to meeting with them. When there is no threat of physical abuse to either adult or to children, meet with the parents together as soon as possible. If conflict escalates, you can always break it down into individual times as needed. The main point is that you will have both parties in your office at the same time. This is symbolic of your belief in co-parenting.

> *Try this*: Arrange two chairs angled slightly away from one another with enough space in between to fit an additional chair. The couch or *love seat* just doesn't apply here. As always, you are simultaneously role modeling your approach by valuing individual separateness as adults/former spouses and togetherness as co-parents. You may prefer to use a round table rather than chairs. This exemplifies a *business-like* atmosphere.

> *Do this*: Use a flip chart to list therapy goals, genograms, the Two-Home Family mission statement, parenting styles, and the co-parenting plan.

And this: Use clinical friendly terms like *parenting together, shared parenting, parenting responsibilities, parent and children rights*, etc. rather than legalese such as *custodial parent, non-custodial parent, residential parent, visitation*, etc. Legal terms should stay in the courtroom. They are negative and counterproductive to the Two-Home Family model. Custodial comes from the word "custodian," meaning janitor (janitor parent; non-janitor parent—the term custody also reminds us of prisoner "in custody"; residential sounds more like an institutional treatment facility; in Alabama we use visitation to refer to the evening before a funeral).

And make sure to: Refer to parents as mother and father rather than former spouse, ex-spouse, etc. Again, you are role modeling your co-parenting emphasis.

Beginning: The Parents Are In

Now is the time to sell your model to them. No matter how much one or both parents want to speak at this point, you must direct the session. Explain to them all the nuts and bolts of how you will proceed. It is important to convey to the parents how much you respect their willingness to meet jointly and that is an indicator of how both of them are committed to doing what is best for their children. Let them know that you have a referral source should either of them want individual and or group counseling to further aid the recovery process.

You are now ready to begin the <u>assessment</u> phase of treatment. The intake form provided you with basic information about their current situation such as legal status and any threat of violent behaviors. At all times, make sure each parent has equal air time to tell you their story and outline their goals for therapy. You will have to be very direct in making sure both adults take turns talking and listening. It is also important to remind them that your role is not to determine *truth or lie*, and that you are not a custody evaluator. Instead, you are the facilitator in aiding their efforts to develop co-parenting plans and find concrete ways to preserve parent-child relationships. In order to succeed with co-parenting plans in place, you must first:

1) Delineate any threat of violence (to any Two-Home Family member).

2) Identify roadblocks that are preventing one or both adults from set-
ting their former roles as marital partners aside and becoming effective co-parents.

3) Determine if children are being used as pawns or go-betweens.

4) Establish the presence of a child-centered vs. a self-centered autobi-
ography of both adults.

5) Assess for any indicators of parental alienation syndrome.

6) Identify all influential players in the divorce drama.

Make sure you do your assessment in all three chapters of the
divorced adults' life: *Family-of-origin, during the marriage, since the
divorce.* Therapists often make the mistake of doing an assessment
where data is based on *present* or *post-divorce* variables only. Of course,
this gleans important information; however, significant data also comes
from both adults' histories: History prior to the marriage and during the
marriage.

During this first session, have the parents sign contracts for treatment
and the release of information form. By the end of this first 90-minute
session, you will have genograms of their homes, treatment goals, and
the beginning of the co-parenting plan.

In-Between

The in-between stage of treatment is approximately sessions two
through six. Sessions two and three are with the parents, the fourth session is with the children (divided into time segments according to child
age), and the fifth and sixth sessions are with each parent and children.

During the second and third sessions, several treatment objectives
must be met. First, you will provide an overview of children's stage and
age of development and how divorce impacts them at each stage. This is
a time to ask the parents to give specific examples of how each of them
has observed their children's reactions to divorce. The adults' stage of
divorce and their own reactions and needs are also explored.

Children give their stories in session four. This is an opportunity for
children to discuss what they need from both parents in both homes to
ease their pain. Children are observed interacting with their mother and
with their father in sessions five and six. This is a time children can tell

each parent privately the things that will enhance their adjustment to divorce.

Some specific interventions that are helpful during sessions five and six include:

1) Create mailboxes for both homes.

2) Write a Two-Home Mission Statement.

3) Outline the roles of all adults in both homes and extended family members.

4) Develop the rules in both homes and explain how those rules are similar and different.

5) Design methods that children can express their frustrations of living between two homes.

6) Learn how change will be addressed as all members move across the life cycle.

The Ending

The ending phase includes session seven when significant others and the parents attend, and the eighth session with all members of both homes. The primary goals of the ending phase are to review the roles of the adults in helping preserve parent-child and extended family member-child relationships. Co-parenting plans are presented by original parents to the significant others in session seven. In the final and eighth session, parents discuss with the children the child-centered decisions they have made, how extended family members will continue to play a vital part in their lives, and the roles of new adult significant others.

For the Children's Sake

The ongoing parental conflict after adults divorce is the primary indicator of children's maladjustment to divorce.

According to the Statistical Abstract of the United States in 2000, one million children become products of parental divorce annually. Of these, about 18.6 million children live in homes primarily governed by one parent; 2/3 of those are with divorced or separated parents. Furthermore, it has been predicted that each year over 3 million children live with grandparents rather than parents—many of those an outcome of divorce. All in all, only about 69 percent of American children reside in the home with both parents on an annual basis. Most children adapt well to the trauma of divorce. In addition, 20–25 percent of these children have serious problems (compared to roughly 10 percent of the children who live with both parents). They are at higher risk for violence, depression, substance abuse, and poor academic performance than children in intact families. Likewise, children from divorced homes are more likely to need mental health professionals than those whose parents stay together. Divorce statistics also indicate that many parents are still bitter toward one another five years after their legal divorce, and one in three children are still involved in that ongoing bitterness.

Children are like adults in that personality, temperament, and character significantly effect how they cope with life's transitions and traumas. However, there are general developmental challenges that also play a part in how children cope with their parents' divorce. These life cycle stages and how divorce impacts them at each stage and age are delineated below.

Infants and Toddlers (Birth to Three Years):

The primary tasks for infants and toddlers are to trust their primary caregivers and to develop secure, attached relationships with them. Young babies require a lot of attention from mothers and fathers.

Consistency in caring for babies is critical. Ideally, the infant needs both parents to feed, bathe, and spend time holding and talking with them.

Divorce challenges for the infant or toddler: Feeling of loss of parent and familiar environment. These negative feelings of loss are diminished when parents can alternate every other day or share time in a single day to care for the little one. The child may cling to both parents during this stage. Encourage parents to be patient and allow their baby to express their feelings in behavioral ways. Many times, babies will act out the anger or hurt they may feel about the change in their family because they don't know how to verbalize emotions.

Here are some basics that will help you help the parents of an infant or toddler.

Recommend that parents:

- Are civil to the other parent in front of the infant/toddler.
- Develop schedules in caring for the baby that allow both parents frequent and regular intervals.
- Gradually move the baby from the familiar home to the second home for overnights.
- Send a toy or other attachment object from one home with the baby to the other parent's home.

Remind parents not to:

- Fight with the other parent in front of the baby.
- Have long periods of time in parenting schedules that result in the infant/toddler being primarily with only one of them for days at a time.

Preschoolers (Three Years to Six Years):

Children in the preschool stage are faced with the developmental task of learning how to do things for themselves and developing their self-identity. Preschool age children are often magical in their way of thinking, they love to explore the environment, and they use fantasy play.

Children who have successfully moved through infancy and toddler-hood are secure, and they trust their parents will meet their physical and safety needs.

Divorce challenges: Secure feelings often are replaced with insecure ones after separation. Clinging to a parent or acting like an infant is not an unusual response to parental divorce for this age group. Magical thinking may include believing the divorce was their fault. For example, a three-year-old states, *"I was bad, and Daddy left."* Because preschool aged children are egocentric, they sometimes do think they are responsi-ble for the actions of others. Likewise, they may try all sorts of behav-iors, such as negative actions, to get the two parents back together.

Direct parents to:

- Tell the child the divorce was not her/his fault.

- Maintain parenting schedules that allow the child to be with each of them every few days.

- Allow their child to embellish stories as his/her way of expression.

- Place a picture of the other parent in the child's bedroom in your home.

- Make a mailbox (e.g., decorate a shoebox) with their preschooler in both homes and put the other parent's name or picture on it. When the child misses the absent parent, he/she can draw a picture, write a letter, etc. Ask the parents to place the mail in the child's bag when making the exchange to the other home.

The School-Age Child (Six Years to 13 Years):

Developing competency, morals, and peer acceptance are critical issues faced by the school-age child. The child at this age needs both par-ents to be dependable and to serve as role models while they face these developmental tasks.

Divorce challenges: The school-age child often feels loyalty conflicts when their parents divorce. They sometimes go through stages of siding with one parent and then the other. Parents have to understand that this is a typical reaction. Make sure parents do not use it as ammunition in a custody battle. Some of these children are ashamed and embarrassed about the divorce and may even try to reconcile their parents. Many children feel deep grief, and they may be overly concerned about how their world is going to change. They may worry about finances, which parent is going to take care of them, and they may even fear a parent will remarry.

Here are some suggestions for parents:

- Let the child know he/she does not have to choose one parent over the other one. Assure her/him that both parents will continue an active role.

- Listen to the child's needs, concerns, and fears. It is important for parents to create an atmosphere that is safe for the child to express frustrations about living between two homes.

- Support the school-age child's relationship with the other parent.

- Allow the child to be a child.

- Attend as many extracurricular activities the child participates in as both parents can. Insure the child that both parents can be there without any concern of either parent creating a "public scene" or embarrassment to him/her.

- Know the school-age child's friends and their parents. To do this, both parents must stay involved with the child on a frequent basis.

- Maintain a civil and courteous relationship with the other parent in front of the child.

- Stay in touch with teachers and ask them to let you know if the child's behaviors or academic performance changes.

- Maintain as much consistency in lifestyle as possible (i.e., same school, neighborhood).

- Be flexible with parenting schedules to help meet the child's social growth.

- Continue with the mailbox idea. Use it to put copies of report cards, activity schedules, etc. that parents receive when their child is with them. This will insure that their child gets the need met of having both parents involved in all aspects of his/her life.

- Use a careful plan to integrate new significant adults into their child's world.

Remind parents <u>not to:</u>

- Bash the other parent in front of their child.

- Judge their child's feelings, concerns or complaints about the divorce.

- Avoid or withdraw from the child.

- Allow their child to withdraw from either of them.

- Expect the child to be the adult and contact a parent if he/she wants to spend time together.

- Put the child in the middle of their divorce war. It is not a child's place to ask the other parent for money, favors, etc.

- Withhold information about their child's school events and activities from the other parent. If they do, they are hurting their child, not just the former spouse.

Adolescents (13 Years to 18 Years):

During this life phase, teenagers are searching for their own individuality by moving away from the family and forming closer relations with their peers.

Divorce challenges: Often, teens worry about one parent and take on the role of the absent parent. Some even form sides with one parent against the other. The divorce may make the adolescent question their own intimate relationships and feel unsure about having a stable and satisfying marriage themselves.

<u>Help parents remember to:</u>

- Stay involved in their teenager's life. Know friends, attend events and activities, and spend private time with him/her.

- Keep the communication line open with their adolescent.

- Coordinate with the other parent to prevent the teen from practicing manipulative behaviors.
- Take care of adult divorce recovery needs with other adults or a caring professional rather than leaning on the adolescent for support.
- Find a mental health professional, youth minister, or other trusting adult for the teen to talk to if she/he doesn't want to talk to the parents about the divorce.
- Be flexible with parenting arrangement to adapt to their teen's developmental needs.
- Allow the adolescent to give input into parenting schedules.

Remind parents not to:
- Expect the adolescent to initiate all conversations with them.
- Condemn, ignore, or attack their teen's thoughts and feelings about the divorce.
- Think that the teen is "old enough" to deal with divorce issues without experiencing any problems.
- Involve their adolescent in their divorce battle.
- Rely on the teen for adult emotional support.
- Use bribery as a means to get the adolescent to choose one side against the other parent.
- Let their teen make all the decisions about spending time with each parent.

College Age/Young Adulthood:

This is a challenging and exciting time as young people work on becoming more autonomous. They struggle with developing intimate relationships, establishing career goals, and comparing a variety of world views to their family-of-origin backgrounds.

Divorce challenges: The college student/young adult may become frustrated with splitting holiday and vacation times. Many of them get tired of trying to please so many adults (both parents, new stepparents, extended family members). They may begin to feel anxious about their own future relationships and marriage.

Remind parents to:

- Give their college age/young adult assurance that both parents will participate in their significant life events such as graduations, celebrations, weddings, etc.

- Allow their child to have an active voice in holiday and vacation plans.

- Encourage continued interactions between the child and both parents.

- Tell the college age/young adult that both of them know divorce is hard on her/him.

- Encourage their child to seek professional help if it is needed.

Words of Wisdom from Children

Below are some direct expressions children of various ages have made in my therapy office. These quotes attest to the importance of why divorcing adults must separate their feelings about one another from their roles as parents.

"I just want Mommy and Daddy to be friends."

Benjamin, age 7 (parents divorced for three years)

"Dear Daddy, I want you to quilt drinking, quilt saying bad things to Mommy when I'm in front of you, go do your best!"

Jennifer, age 10 (parents divorced for six months)

"My mamma says my daddy is real mean and I shouldn't be nice to him."

Timothy, age 8 (divorce in-process)

"Daddy told me that me and him are going to California, and I won't ever have to see my mamma because she ain't good for me."

Justin, age 6 (divorce in-process)

"My mom is so sad and I am the only person she talks to. See, I am tougher than she is so I have to be strong to help her."

Melissa, age 13 (parents divorced for 10 months)

"I hate it when he questions me about Mom's social life. He knows she is dating John. But he can't stand it that she is happy. He expects me to tell him every time Mom and John have a date. I don't want to talk to him or have dinner with him anymore."

> Lauren, age 16 (parents divorced for four years)

"I don't want Daddy to go."

> Matthew, age 5 (divorce in-process)

"I just don't want to be with him right now. My mom needs me. I finally had enough of his criticism. My mom has a lawyer who is going to get it changed so I can live with her. He thinks this is her idea, but it is mine. I want to be with my mom all the time."

> Lawrence, age 15 (parents divorced for 10 years)

"I feel like a rubber band…Mamma pulls me to her and Daddy pulls me to him."

> Erica, age 12 (parents divorced for two years)

"My own book about DEVORCE:

It's hard being the only child especially if your parents are DEVORCED! The older you get, you'll get used to it, as you get older. It kind of gets on my nervers driving back and forth, back and forth to my dad's house and my mom's house and it is not fare having your parents DEVORCED! If I had to chose to live with my mom or dad, I would go live with my grandma and granddaddy and never go back! I hate my parents being DEVORCED!"

> Caroline, age 9 (parents divorced three years)

"My Rules:

1. Don't put me in the middle.
2. Quit arguing.
3. Quit saying bad things.
4. Talk polite to each other/about each other.
5. All parents (step and real) come to my activities.

6.   Braeck bad habits like smoking and drinking."

Caroline, age 9 (same as above)

"I called my dad and asked him to come to my graduation party. He said he would love to as long as my mom didn't bring that S.O.B. she is married to. I called my mom and invited her and she said she couldn't come if my dad brought that whore he is living with. I told both of them that my fiancé's parents were going to be my new parents and neither of them was going to come to my graduation or my wedding! I finally had enough! They have been divorced for ten years, and they still hate each other."

Alan, age 26

"When my first baby was born my mother refused to come to the hospital, because my father was going to be there. I thought I would get used to it, but it has been 18 years and now that I have children it spills over onto them. My parents live close by one another, and since I live away it would be nice if they would take the kids to each other's home in the summer, but they won't. I have to coordinate all of that. My kids have started to pick up on how weird things are."

Julie, age 34

"The thing I am most sick of is trying to please everybody. I have to please daddy and my step-mom when I am there, mamma and my step-dad when I stay with them. And then there are my grandparents. Sometimes, I just don't want to go home for vacations or holidays."

Jimmy, age 20 (parents divorced for four years)

"Daddy and my step-mom had a new baby and it is a girl. I don't want to go to his house anymore. I'm scared I am not his little princess anymore."

Laura, age 16 (parents divorced for two years)

Helping Parents Help Their Children

A family system, Two-Home Family Approach to divorce is an effective way to show parents how to help their children. The above is an outline of specific child needs at certain developmental stages of life and some direct quotes from children of divorce. Below are some basic parenting principles for divorced parents regardless of child age:

Parenting Do's:

- Spend regular, consistent time with children.

- Know the developmental age/stage issues, challenges, and needs.

- Maintain familiar routine as much as possible (limit the losses).

- Be flexible and adaptable.

- Maintain children's interactions with extended family members.

- Have a careful plan to integrate new significant others to children.

- Attend children's activities (i.e., sports, arts, church) and visit schools.

- Keep commitments and promises made to children.

- Speak directly to the other parent rather than having the child as the go-between.

- Pay attention to tone when talking to the other parent in front of the children.

- Make sure the children know the divorce was not their fault.

- Get adult support rather than relying on children for emotional help.

- Receive help from a family systems Two-Home Family divorce expert.

Parenting Don'ts:

- Don't ignore or avoid children when upset with the other parent.
- Don't manipulate, pressure, or lie in order to make children take sides.
- Don't ask children whom they want to live with.
- Don't expose children to your arguments, abusive behavior, or conflicts.
- Don't rely on children for emotional support.
- Don't ask children to read legal documents about the divorce.
- Don't bash the other parent in front of the children.
- Don't force new significant others onto children.
- Don't bash other parent's extended family members.
- Don't be rigid.

Adult Stuff

Until recent years, individuals divorcing one another have primarily utilized the legal system alone to air personal grievances. Of course, the degree of the legal battle often was dictated by who had the best lawyer, the most money and power, and who appeared to be the better parent. The battle also had a lot to do with which adult was the "dumper" vs. the "dumpee." Even though this process continues in many courtrooms, there is now much more legal support for adults to *act right* in some collaborative manner in an effort to stop the messy aftermath of divorce. Many legal systems mandate seminars geared around parenting together after divorce and some even require that a formal parenting plan become part of the final decree. Others also have restrictions on the geographical mobility of a parent with primary care of the children.

As previously noted, one-third to one-half of former spouses maintain intense anger toward one another years after the divorce is final. As mental health professionals, we are aware that adults may replace spouses at any time but children cannot replace original parents. Our hope is that the current legal movement will serve in decreasing the continued hostility between former spouses for the sake of the children. By using a Two-Home Family approach, we are in a good position to help the adults divorce the marriage while they maintain co-parental relationships.

To successfully sell the Two-Home Family model to the adults, it is imperative to address the *roadblocks* parents face before reaching the ultimate goal of co-parenting. To do so, therapists must show they are not only "child-centered," but "adult-centered," as well. A general overview of what divorce is like for the adults is presented below, and as you will see, these stages of recovery can thwart efforts to parent together.

Six Stages of Divorce

Paul Bohannon described stages of divorce for adults in his 1970 book *Divorce and After*. In his model, at least six things are happening to adults during divorce. These may occur in random order with varying intensities, but all adults face these six experiences. The first is the emotional stage, and it is during this time that one or both spouses withhold emotional intimacy from the marriage. One partner may have started that process long before the legal stage, or when the judge signs the decree. The economic phase often causes great legal battles as the adults separate liabilities and assets. Adults also go through a community stage as they grieve old relations and begin new ones. During the psychic stage, each adult begins the movement from a "we" to a "me" in search of autonomy. Finally, the co-parental phase requires parents to separate mother and father responsibilities in rearing the children.

The therapist's goal is to assist the adults in the co-parental stage with the Two-Home Family model. To do so, it is emphasized that co-parenting is a *business-like* relationship—children are the products of that partnership. When one or both adults remain stuck in one of the other stages of divorce, further treatment targeting the symptoms is necessary before the therapist can move forward with co-parenting. These roadblocks are presented below.

Roadblock #1: Economics

If economic disputes are ongoing, one or both partners may not be able to proceed to the co-parenting stage and thus are not yet good candidates for a Two-Home Family model. Other adults, however, are able to compartmentalize divorce and leave the economic stuff with a mediator, financial adviser, or attorney. As needed, make appropriate referrals to help the adults resolve those differences.

Roadblock #2: The Community

Sometimes, family and friends are over-involved in the divorce process with one or both of the adults. It may be helpful to have both adults make a commitment that they will quit talking to friends and family members about the ugly stuff going on with their divorcing spouse. Instead, they will focus on themselves and how they are going to establish a new climate in their social support network. Family and friends can then be resources to help the adult rediscover him/herself. The community stage of divorce can also present grief issues when adults no longer have contact with the partner's extended family/friendship network. Have the adults talk to one another about this in session so that they can come up with some ways to heal the pain.

Roadblock #3: The Psychic

True mental illness may prevent an adult from separating marriage from parenting. Refer these adults to a psychologist or psychiatrist for diagnosis and treatment. Collaborate with other providers as you develop your Two-Home Family treatment plan.

Roadblock #4: Emotions

The emotional divorce refers to the *continued attachment between former spouses*. Attachment is a normal outcome of strong, close relationships and can result in either positive or negative feelings toward the attachment figure. Letting go of this attachment is easier said than done and it may continue long after legal and economic stages. Additionally, the emotional process is never on the same time zone for both adults. Usually one partner became disillusioned long before the other was aware that problems were significant or divorce was imminent. A successful Two-Home Family occurs when the adults divorce the marriage and spend energy and resources on co-parenting. Facilitating this process may take several sessions. The important thing to keep in mind is that closure of the marriage has to occur before the adults can move forward and develop the *business-like partnership* around parenting.

Strategies to help divorcing adults sever marital bonds:

In some situations, detachment may be facilitated if both partners are in a joint-therapy session. In other cases, both individuals will require independent counseling. Regardless of the format, the following may help:

- Each partner has to own responsibility for the good, the bad, and the ugly that occurred during the marriage. Ask the partner for forgiveness if warranted.

- Acknowledge when the relationship took a turn from an intimate friendship to a distant or bitter acquaintance. Use a timeline on the flipchart to depict significant life events.

- Set new life goals. Make sure the Two-Home Family model is included.

- Create new traditions for special days, holidays, vacations, etc.

- Write a good-bye letter to the marriage. Read this to the other partner in session.

- Promise to be patient with the self and introduce change slowly.

- Join a support group of other divorcing adults.

- Seek individual counseling when needed.

- Give permission to grieve one's own way. Grief is a unique experience.

Roadblock #5: Parental Alienation Syndrome (PAS)

Dr. Richard Gardner defined PAS:

"PAS is a distinctive family response to divorce in which the child becomes aligned with one parent and preoccupied with unjustified and/or exaggerated denigration of the other, target parent."

Parental alienation syndrome destroys parent-child relationships and is psychologically harmful to the targeted child and to the targeted parent. Parents who attempt to alienate children from the other parent often are bitter about the pain experienced in the marriage. Negative attachment feelings toward the former spouse have been amplified by the divorce. Vindictiveness is not the only motivator; a goal for financial gain (i.e., obtain full primary "custody" to increase child support payments) may be behind the alienation efforts.

In your assessment, make sure you gather data from all family members and carefully connect the dots that might lead to PAS. Keep in mind that during the early stages of divorce recovery many parents make negative comments about the other parent. In PAS cases, however, comments and behaviors increasingly become more hostile. The following will assist you in your evaluation:

Indicators of an Alienating Parent (parent who seeks to alienate child from other parent):

- Is influenced by a new significant other.

- Has intrusive parents.

- Threatens to abduct the child.

- Refuses other parent contact with the child.

- Prevents other parent's extended family from contacting child.

- Sabotages gifts, cards, and messages to child from other parent.

- Accuses other parent of being abusive to child.

Indicators of a Targeted Child (parent is alienating child from other parent):

- Child makes irrational excuses to avoid target parent.

- Child glorifies one parent and demonizes the other.

- Child has unjustified anger and hatred for target parent's extended family.

- Child shows no remorse for speaking negatively about the target parent.

- Child uses words and phrases like those made by alienating parent.

- Child argues that he/she has not been influenced by the aligned parent.

PAS has to stop before you can move toward helping the parents develop a workable co-parenting relationship. It is also important to counsel all family members when PAS has been identified.

Counseling the Child:

- Gather information about the relationship the child had with the target parent during the marriage. Sometimes it is helpful for a child to bring photos of the two of them to session.

- Help identify the child's cognitive distortions. It is illogical to state that one parent is perfect and the other can do nothing right.

- Assure the child that it is okay to have a relationship with both parents.

- Meet with the child and both parents in concurrent sessions.

Counseling the Parents:

- Boldly state that the parent who is alienating the child from the other parent is hurting the child.

- Let the alienating parent know that his/her future relationship with the child is being jeopardized.

- Encourage the target parent not to give up.

- Direct the target parent to increase his/her social support network.

- Help the target parent develop ways to stay on the offensive and not on the defensive (the parent-relationship stays in focus as the primary goal).

There are times when it may be necessary to confront the alienating parent with questions such as:

- Do you want to have a relationship with your child when she is an adult?

- Do you want your grown child to bring your grandchildren to visit you when you are old?

- Do you believe it is truly in the best interest of your child to never see his father again?

- What if you were no longer mad at your ex—then would she be a good mother to your child?

- How was it that your child's father was a good parent when you were married, and now that you are divorced, he is so horrible?

Keep in mind that in some cases, both parents are trying to alienate the other parent! One may target one child, the other another child. Always proceed with caution when you see alliances between a child and a parent. Act fast to get the target child and target parent in a joint session. I have found court orders are often necessary to get these families to follow my Two-Home Family protocol. I don't hesitate to phone one or both of the party's attorneys and ask if a motion could be filed to get all members from both homes in therapy as quickly as possible. I give general rationale to the attorneys: "*I am concerned about the children and the relationships between the children and the parents. It is to the children's benefit that the legal system assists me in requiring everyone to come see me."*

There has been some controversy over the use of the term *Parental Alienation Syndrome*. Some scholars argue that if it is really a syndrome, then it should be included in the DSM-IV as a diagnosis. To address this concern, I do not use the term in my evaluation reports. Instead, I use words such as "sabotage," "destroy," and "end" when referring to patterns of behavior. When I do use the word "alienate," I do not call it a "syndrome." As a therapist, whether or not PAS is a clinical diagnosis is of little concern to me. What is important is that for years I have witnessed vengeful behaviors by a parent where it was apparent the ultimate goal was to make the other parent quit on the relationship with the child. And, I am grateful that the late Dr. Gardner labeled this tragedy and gave us criteria for its occurrence.

Roadblock #6: Domestic Violence: Overt vs. Covert

Overt

Review the intake forms both adults completed prior to the first session. If one partner indicated abuse, meet with the parents separately to gather detailed information about the violence. Find a domestic violence expert you can make referrals to if you are unsure of how to work in this specialty area.

Covert

Sometimes victims of domestic violence do not indicate abuse on the intake form, but patterns may evolve that make you suspicious. Domestic violence is the physical, emotional, mental, or sexual abuse of one partner toward the other. Pay attention to the following in your interviews as the behaviors may support your hunch that abuse is a threat:

- Dominating, intimidating behaviors by one partner and timid responses by the other.

- One party agrees with whatever the other party says about parenting, even though it may be in neither her/his best interest nor the children's.

Sometimes divorce brings out the dark, ugly monster that looks like abuse, and behaviors exhibited may be a result of the divorce rather than true abuse. However, if you see indications that you believe constitute abuse, then separate the couple and ask very specifically about the role of violence in the marriage and family. The following questions will help you:

- Has abuse occurred during your marriage?

- Will you tell me exactly who has done what?

- How long has this been happening?

- Has it happened since you separated?

- Have any threats or abusive behaviors been directed at the children?

- Can you see that the way you talk to your child's mother/father is controlling and abusive?

- Will you be able to maintain civility and calmness when you sit down in here with your child's father/mother and discuss parenting?

Many couples can work together if mild or moderate domestic violence was present during the marriage but has been absent since separation. In more severe cases, it is best to treat them separately or refer them to a domestic violence specialist.

Roadblock #7: Child Abuse

If a parent maintains that the other parent is abusive or is a threat to a child, then you are obligated to explore the allegation thoroughly. Sometimes a parent lies about child abuse (physical, emotional, mental, and sexual) and uses it as a weapon in the parental alienation war. If you do suspect an allegation is warranted, make the appropriate reports and discontinue the Two-Home Family treatment until an investigation is completed.

Parenting Together After the Marriage Ends

Once the above roadblocks have been addressed head-on, the Two-Home Family therapist is ready to begin working on preserving the parent-child relationships. This process begins with evaluating the <u>parenting style</u> of each adult.

Parenting Styles

Clinicians are aware of the three common types of parenting that have been outlined in textbooks and popular literature for decades. I have modified the terms to relate to laypeople in a humorous way:

❖ *Hippie Parents*

Hippie homes have a major rule: There are no rules. Children and adults cross over each other's boundaries at any time. Many children who are products of hippie homes are able to rise above that environment and become responsible citizens. Others, however, do not grow up, become responsible or leave home. As a matter of fact, they may choose to stay home and bring grandchildren into the home for their parents to raise as little hippies.

❖ *Hitler Parents*

Hitler homes have very rigid rules. So rigid that eight-year olds and sixteen-year olds have the same bedtime. Many of these children leave family stuff behind and are at peace with the world as adults. Others are angry, rebellious, and may have even run away from home as teens.

❖ *Huxtabel Parents (or Hero Parents)*

Huxtabel (taken from the ideal parents portrayed in the Bill Cosby show) homes are structured but flexible. They set rules to meet individual members' needs according to stage and age. Children from Huxtabel homes learn to face the natural consequences of their actions. They are typically successful and happy in adulthood.

Try this:

Use a continuum on the flip chart and draw the three parenting styles with Hippie on the far left, Huxtabel in the middle, and Hitler on the far right. Now draw gradations along the continuum and ask each parent to plot where they were as parents during the marriage and where they are now. It is often helpful for parents to talk about wanting to be accepted as a good, caring parent and it is okay to differ in many ways from one another. At the same time, children benefit from having some consistency in major rules between the two homes. The key word is <u>accepting</u> one another as parents and allowing each other to parent his/her own way.

Next, the quality of the co-parenting interactions is measured.

Co-Parenting

The major function of the family unit is to meet the needs of its individual members and to maintain its structure and organization. Divorce forces the family to adapt to rapid and profound structural and organizational changes. Divorce can terminate the relationship between former spouses when children are not involved. With children in the picture, however, it is desirable that the adults develop workable co-parental interactions. This requires the parents to figure out the logistics of coordinating children's lives between two homes.

We know that during marriage many adults were able to parent together without any formal written agreements. We also know that many parents argued frequently about parenting differences. The same phenomenon is present after divorce. Some parents are able to develop co-parenting relationships like those delineated initially by clinical scholar, Constance Ahrons. These types may be either <u>cooperative, conflicted,</u> or <u>disengaged</u> co-parental interactions.

When parents are cooperative, our work is much easier! They share parenting, support one another as an equal partner in the co-parental relationship, regardless of their feelings toward the other person as an individual. This cooperative, business-like parenting relationship reduces the children's sense of loss and alleviates the overload faced by a primary parent. When parents are willing to set aside old marital agendas, the Two-Home Family therapist aids the development of a <u>Cooperative Co-parenting Plan.</u>

Until recently, many mental health professionals saw the conflicted or disengaged co-parental styles as hopeless. Instead of helping the adults move out of those positions, they often gave up and sent the individuals and/or children to individual counselors. From a family systems perspective, however, we know that many of these adults are able to forgive and heal to the degree that they may not be cooperative partners but are able to develop <u>Parallel Co-Parenting Plans.</u>

Remember, you must first build both parents up before you can expect the parents to build two homes for their children's sake! It takes both parents to build a two-home, post-divorce family that is governed by a cooperative co-parenting system. Sometimes, one or both parents refuse because of continued hostility they aren't ready to rid themselves of. They may still be child-centered and want effective parent-child relationships and even though they refuse to interact directly, they can sometimes build parallel co-parenting relationships. The cooperative co-parents have fluid and malleable boundaries. Parallel parents have boundaries that are rigid and impermeable. Both types can be actively involved in their children's lives. A downfall to the parallel co-parents may surface when children are adolescents. At that time, the teens may manipulate the parents when questioned about their whereabouts (e.g., regarding one weekend a teen said to his mother, "I was at Dad's"; and to his father he reported: "I was at Mom's.").

Below, the major ingredients of developing either type of co-parenting will be outlined. Then, the unique characteristics of each will follow.

Developing a Co-Parenting Plan

All co-parenting plans must:

- Be developed by the parents. A plan written by a therapist will have much less meaning to the parents and is less likely to be adhered to.

- Mandate parents as the CEOs, while the children are children.

- Require that parents live within a reasonable proximity of one another so the child has access to both.

- Be based on the developmental needs of the child (e.g., flexibility, adaptability, attachment, and child's sense of time).

- Include a time and means once a week that parents can discuss the children ("staff meeting").

- Open telephone time with each parent (as long as talk is not self-centered or negative).

- A picture of the other parent in child's room.

- A "mailbox" in each home (to relay to the other parent: child schedules, report card copies, notes, pictures, etc. from child to the other parent). The mailbox is made by each parent separately with the child. Some decorate shoe boxes, etc. to make this mailbox. Parents agree not to use this as their means of communicating negativity to the other parent!

- A calendar displayed where the child can see the schedule when he/she will be at the home with mother or father.

- Allow each parent to parent his/her own way.

- Alternate morning, afternoon, and evening pick-up and drop-off from school and other activities whenever possible to reduce separation anxiety and increase two-parent involvements.

- A careful plan will be used to introduce new adult significant others to the children.

- Extended family members will remain vital roles in the lives of the children.

- When economics allow, children maintain the involvement in extracurricular activities as they did prior to divorce.

- Parents agree on the educational system and medical care of children.

<u>Sample Co-Parenting Plan</u> *(will be signed by both parents and witnessed by the Two-Home Family Therapist))*

The Jones Two-Home Family Cooperative Co-parenting Plan

1. I commit to being child-centered.

2. I recognize the importance of living close by my former spouse, for our children's sake.

3. I will not belittle, criticize, or communicate anything negative (by word, body language, or facial expression) about my former spouse in front of our children.

4. I may not agree with my former spouse about all parenting issues, but promise not to judge or condemn him/her as long as abuse is absent.

5. When I see my former spouse in the presence of our children, I will speak and act kindly, respectfully, and graciously.

6. If I am dealing with a conflict that may elicit negative emotions with my former spouse, I will speak or meet him/her when the children are not present.

7. I will make every effort to give undivided attention to my children on a consistent basis by listening to them, doing fun things with them, and giving parental support to the best of my ability.

8. I will keep my dating life out of my children's life totally during the early stages of divorce recovery, understanding that with each new face they see they potentially suffer another loss and may even feel my love is another threatened loss.

9. I will tell my children I love them everyday or as often as I see them and will reassure nothing will ever change that. I will use touch and physical affection as other ways to express my love to them.

10. I will not use my children as the go-between with questions or information to or about my former spouse.

11. I will make an attempt to agree with my former spouse on issues of conflict pertaining to the children and will obtain professional help if necessary.

12. I will not say anything negative about my former spouse to friends, family members, or any person in the presence of my children.

13. I will seek what is best for my children in all I do, knowing at times that will be very difficult and require self-sacrifice.

14. I will make every effort to cooperate, share, and support my former spouse as the other parent and treat our co-parenting relationship

like a "business" one rather than an emotionally charged or intimate one.

_____	_____	_____
Parent	Parent	Witness

Sample Parallel Co-Parenting Plan _(will be signed by both parents and the Two-Home Family Therapist)_)

Same as above with added statements such as:

15. The conflict with my former spouse is so high that I recognize its potential to harm my children. Therefore, I agree to a third party as a mediator for pick-ups, drop-offs, and sharing information about our children's schedules and activities.

16. When my former spouse and I contact one another via emails, voice mails, etc., I agree to adult privacy and will not allow my children to have access to any of the information.

17. I understand that our children want us both at their extracurricular activities and events. I will stay clear from my former spouse and will do everything I can to keep the atmosphere pleasant for our children.

18. I will not bring our children into the war I have with my former spouse.

19. I will not offer bribes to our children to make me appear as the best or most desirable parent.

_____	_____	_____
Parent	Parent	Witness

Two-Home Family Mission Statement*

It is helpful to employ an intervention that requires parents and children in session together while writing their Two-Home Family Mission Statement. The therapist writes the statement down on the flipchart as the family members dictate its content. It is important that you make sure all family members have an opportunity to provide input and that the statement is written to address individual and systemic needs. The mission statement may be included in the formal "Two-Home Family Evaluation" for the legal system.

Questions that may help stimulate the process for family members to write their mission statement include:

- What is the main function of your two homes?

- What are your goals for two homes?

- What are the responsibilities of each family member?

- What kind of relationships do you desire to have with one another?

Here are two sample mission statements written by Two-Home Families:

Our Two-Home Family mission is to make sure that the parents are civil in front of the children. In our two homes, the children are not caught in the middle of the adults' divorce battles. Children and parents are free to love and nurture one another without the other parent interfering.

~

The Smith Two-Home Family mission statement:

- *To allow both parents to be actively involved in the children's lives.*

- *To maintain a child-centered philosophy.*

- *To be responsible for keeping adult stuff with the adults.*

- *To let children be children at all times.*
- *To make both homes pleasant, peaceful and a joy to be in.*

*This was adapted from the work of Stephen Covey (1997) (The Seven Habits of Highly Effective Families).

Summary

There are times at termination when co-parenting plans have been signed and mission statements written when you will feel elated. Just watching the process is phenomena and it makes you wish all families undergoing the trauma of divorce could get to this point. But all families will not. During those times, therapists may become disappointed and even feel deflated. It is then that we have to remind ourselves that we must keep on trying!!

One way I evaluate myself is by asking my PLE question at the end of each session and at the termination of therapy:

"P"—Was I professional?
"L"—Was I legal?
"E"—Was I ethical?

If I can answer yes to those, then I have done my best with all cases. Divorced families bring with them a very specific evaluative and accountability question, however:

Did I do everything I could possibly do to get both parents in sessions?

Good luck in your efforts to serve families during a very painful time in the lives of all their members.

Appendices

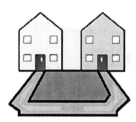

Two-Home Families:

A Step-by-Step Approach for Preserving Parent-Child Relationships After the Marriage Ends

Dr. Brenda Dozier

Did you know that ongoing parental conflict is the number one indicator of children's maladjustment to divorce?

Dr. Dozier's
Two-Home Family model addresses that question and much more...

- Detaching from an ex-spouse
- Parental alienation syndrome
- Cooperative Co-parenting
- Parallel Co-parenting
- Child Developmental Stage/Age
- Violence Screening

In 8 - 12 sessions, all members in both homes are evaluated and treated. The primary goal of the Two-Home Family model is to preserve parent-child relationships and to help parents develop effective co-parenting plans.

Even though 1/3 to 1/2 of the divorced adults in America are still hostile five years after divorce is legal, most of them want to do what is best for their children. Others wrongfully involve their children in their divorce battles. Dr. Dozier's Two-Home Family Approach will tackle the most difficult separating or divorcing couples.

For more information or to schedule an initial consultation please call:
Dr. Brenda Dozier
334-821-3631
Auburn Family Therapy
118 N. Ross Suite 6
PO Box 2056
Auburn, AL 36831

Two-Home Family Intake Form

Please complete this entire form. Thank you.

1. Your Name_____

2. Birth Date_____ Age_____

3. Address_____
    City_____ State_____ Zip_____
    Home Phone_____ Cell Phone_____

4. Work Place_____
    Address_____ Phone_____
    Position_____ How Long?_____

5. Educational Status _____

6. Marriage Date_____ Where_____

7. Separated?_____ If so, date of separation_____

8. Divorced?_____ If so, date of final decree_____

9. Children's full names   Birth Date   Age   School
    _____
    _____
    _____

10. List previous marriages (please give name of former spouse and
    when and where marriage ended)
    _____
    _____
    _____

11. List names and ages of children from former marriages and resi-
    dence of each
    _____
    _____
    _____

12. Do you wish to reconcile?_____

13. Are you currently in therapy or counseling? _____
    If so, with who?_____

14. Attorney's Name_____ Phone_____
    Address_____ Fax_____

15. Mediator's Name_____ Phone_____
    Fax:_____ Address_____

Confidential—Intake Form 2

The potential for any violence must be assessed before beginning the
Two-Home Family Work

1. During your marriage, did your spouse abuse you in any
   way?_____
   Please describe_____
   _____
   _____
   _____

2. Since the separation/divorce (if applicable), has your spouse abused
   you?_____
   Please explain_____
   _____
   _____
   _____

3. Since separation or divorce, has your spouse threatened harm to
   you?_____
   _____
   _____
   _____
   _____
   _____
   _____

4. Are you comfortable to meet in sessions with your
   spouse?_____
   Explain_____
   _____
   _____

5. Has your spouse abused your child(ren)?_____
   If yes, please describe_____
   _____
   _____
   _____
   _____

6. Do you think your spouse is a danger to your child(ren)?_____

_____

_____

_____

_____

Two-Home Family Therapy
Agreement

The primary goal of the Two-Home Family Therapy model is to preserve parent-child relationships by decreasing parental conflict and developing workable co-parenting plans.

Both parents agree to participate in eight-12 sessions with the undersigned Two-Home Family Therapist. The parties understand that the sessions will be structured and organized by the therapist and changes will be made as needed. Children, extended family members, new spouses, and significant others will be included as the therapist deems appropriate.

The parents agree to pay the therapist_____ per 90-minute session. Payment will be made at the end of each session.

_____

Date

_____

Parent

_____

Parent

_____

Therapist

Multiple Authorization to Release and Exchange Information

Name_____

Address_____

City_____State_____Zip_____

Name_____

Address_____

City_____State_____Zip_____

This authorizes the undersigned therapist to release and exchange information concerning our divorce situation with the following parties: (e.g., attorneys, teachers, new spouses, extended family members)

	Name	Telephone
Attorney	_____	_____
Attorney	_____	_____
Others:	_____	_____

_____

_____

_____

_____

We understand that all client information is confidential and my records, with respect to alcohol and drug abuse, are protected under the Federal Confidentiality Regulations and cannot be disclosed without my written consent unless provided for in the regulations. I understand that either of us may revoke this authorization at any time, except to the extent that action has already been taken to comply with it. Without our expressed revocation, this authorization will automatically expire at the termination of treatment by our Two-Home Family Therapist at Auburn Family Therapy.

_____	_____	_____
Client	Client	Witness

Confidential
Two-Home Family Evaluation

This is not a custody evaluation. It is a Two-Home Family Evaluation that centers on preserving parent-child relationships and focuses on meeting individual members' needs in both post-divorce family homes.

Client Family Name: Parents: John Doe
                                  Jane Doe

               Children: Susie (8-4-90)
                       Cora (7-20-91)
                       Bobbi (2-23-92)
                       Mary (6-16-94)

Court: Circuit Court of Chambers County, Alabama; Case #CR-94-2, 3.01, 3.02

Dates of Evaluation: 10-12-02; 10-15-02; 10-20-02; 11-02-02; 11-13-02; 11-16-02; 11-21-02; 12-06-02
Date of Report: 01-8-03

Source and Reason for Referral: Circuit Court of Chambers County, Alabama, ordered family to therapy in an effort to resolve current "custody" issue.

Relevant Background Information: Parents divorced in 1996, and the mother was awarded primary care of the children during the nine-month school year and the father responsible for parenting every other weekend and during the summer months. Since the legal divorce, there have been times of cooperative co-parenting and times of hostility and a lack of cooperativeness between the parents. Much of the difficulty in shared parenting responsibilities appears to be associated with the physical distance between the Two-Home Family: the father lives in Somewhere, Florida, and the mother in Anymore, Alabama—about six hours apart.

The father is remarried with one child, and his current wife's two children from her previous marriage are also in the home. The mother remains single with no other children in the home.

Both parents received counseling services prior to the divorce, and the mother reports some continued services for divorce adjustment after the decree was final. The mother was also treated for alcohol abuse in 1986. Neither parent is prescribed medication for any physical or psychological difficulties.

Behavioral Observations: All clients (both parents and the four children) were cooperative and responsive to the evaluative process. No unusual behaviors were observed.

Intellectual and Cognitive Functioning: The mother is a medical doctor, and the father is an elementary school educator. The children are all honor students and all members of both homes appeared to function around the average to above-average range of intellectual functioning. Vocabulary, fund of knowledge, insight, and judgment in all parties were consistent with that estimate.

Personality Functioning: All clients denied both hallucinations and suicidal/homicidal ideations, and none of them indicated delusions or looseness of associations. All were oriented to time, place, person, and situation.

Presenting Issues: The Two-Home Family reported to Dr. Brenda Dozier for assistance in reaching resolution regarding where the children would live during the academic school year. Dr. Dozier has specialized in "Two-Home Families" for over 15 years, and she helps parents help their children cope with divorce issues by developing co-parenting plans that are "child" centered rather than "adult-self" centered. Not only does she work directly with parents and children, but she serves as an expert witness for court systems and teaches professional seminars on the topic.

The father reported that the children want to live in his home during the school year because they have been worried about their mother's alcohol use/abuse. The mother voiced that she thinks the father wants the children three-fourths of the year as a means to increase his family income via child support payments.

Cora and Bobbi did report that they had some concerns about their mother's alcohol consumption. In December, both girls stated that they were less anxious about their mother's drinking since they had all been in therapy. They were unsure if their mother was practicing "closet drinking" habits. Susie and Mary consistently reported that they had no concerns in either of their homes, and they just wished their parents would quit fighting about it.

Summary and Recommendations: Chronic parental/legal battles over the amount of time children spend with each of the parents causes distress to the children who are victims of divorce. All four children in this case perceived that they were often caught in the middle of their parents' war. The two middle daughters formed an alliance with the father and the oldest and youngest with the mother. These strategies could be the children's way of trying to fix the family problems and maintain loyalty to both parents. On a more positive note, in light of the ongoing parental war, the four girls seem to be quite balanced academically, athletically, socially, spiritually, and artistically. All of them are quite accomplished.

These four children need both parents, and they need to feel secure with having two homes even with the distance between the two. In order to effectively design this Two-Home model, the parents must develop an effective co-parenting plan that puts their children's needs first. Prior to a written, formal, cooperative co-parenting plan, it is my strong recommendation that the following occur:

1. The children should not be subjected to any open court testimony (this would make them choose one parent over the other).

2. The girls return to counseling sessions once a month with this therapist.

3. The mother receives an outpatient evaluation and recommendation concerning her alcohol use/abuse from a substance abuse expert and that report is shared with Dr. Dozier.

Once those three recommendations are followed, it is requested that the court mandate the parents attend co-parenting sessions with Dr. Dozier until a cooperative co-parenting plan is written.

Brenda Dozier, Ph.D., LMFT, LPC
Two-Home Family Therapist

Confidential
Two-Home Family Evaluation

This is not a custody evaluation. It is a Two-Home Family evaluation that centers on preserving parent-child relationships following divorce.

Client Family: Parents: John Doe
                            Mary Doe
     Children: Billy Doe (DOB: 1/19/90-13 years)
                 Kale Doe (DOB: 6/20/94-9 years)
Dates of Evaluation: March 2003–present
Date of Report: November 4, 2003

<u>Source and Reason for Referral:</u> Both parents were referred by their respective attorneys. A court order from the Family Court Judge, Lee County, Alabama, mandated all family members receive evaluation and treatment.

<u>Relevant Background Information:</u> Parents have been divorced for four years.

Father reports that the mother is trying to destroy the relationships between both sons and him. The mother argues that the father bashes her in front of the boys. On several scheduled times, the father went to pick the boys up from the mother's home, and no one was there. The mother believed she had reason to take the boys away because the father had threatened to leave the state with them. The mother tape-recorded telephone conversations between the father and the boys. During the talks, the father did call the mother names (*"bitch," "whore"*) and was obviously coaching them in ways to leave their mother's home permanently. For example, the father said to the oldest son: *"You have got to help me get ya'll away from her. Did 'he' spend the night with her again? What do you mean you went to sleep? I need you to watch what that bitch is doing. Do you understand? Ok, son. Don't let me down."*

<u>Behavioral Observations:</u> Both adults had difficulty being in the therapy office together. When one of them would begin to outline goals for their children, the other would turn it into a personal attack. The oldest son appeared to be coached by the father and made statements that were identical to the words the father had spoken about the mother. Examples

include: *"She makes us hangout with her boyfriend. She is never home. We stay by ourselves all the time. I hate her. She is a whore."* The youngest son was much more open and spontaneous, but he mimicked his older brother in repeating that their goal was to be with their father all of the time.

Based on initial observations and clinical interviews, it appears that both the father and mother are attempting to sabotage the relationship between both boys and the other parent. Apparently, these behaviors have gone on for the entire four years since legal divorce. If they continue, both boys are at risk of psychological and social disturbances.

The Sessions: The father acknowledged how wrong it was for him to use the boys the way he did. It is important to note that the time the telephone calls were recorded was immediately after the father went to pick the boys up for a week-long camping trip and the mother had absconded with them to her boyfriend's. The father stated that he knew his vindictiveness was wrong, but that he was reacting to his frustration of packing the week's camping gear and feeling so helpless when he went to get his children and the gates were locked and he could not find them.

In session with the boys, the father apologized and admitted that his behavior was wrong, and that he would not try to make either of them form sides with him again.

There were times the parents gave the appearance they would continue to share parenting and take on a more cooperative spirit with one another. Unfortunately, those periods were short-lived. One or both adults would sabotage the other's ability to cooperate. These actions indicate that the adults have not severed their emotional attachment from the marital relationship and do not seem motivated to do so. It is important that divorced adults leave the emotional bond as marital partners behind in order to move forward as effective cooperative co-parents to their children. Research data reveals that about one-half of the divorced adults with children are able to do so. The other half remains hostile and bitter for many years—some even a lifetime.

Since the actions displayed by John and Mary indicate little-to-no desire to sever old painful allegiances to one another and become cooperative co-parents, I recommend that they work with me independently to develop an alternative divorced parenting relationship I have developed: Parallel Co-parenting. Under this parenting arrangement, the adults will not speak directly (i.e., face-to-face; telephone). Instead, they will agree on a neutral third party to serve as the go-between to pick up/drop off the children, relay messages concerning parenting, etc. It is imperative that they both agree to attend sporting events their boys participate in, but they let the boys know they will not speak to one another, harass one another, nor will they prevent the other parent from attending.

<u>Recommendations:</u> Because of the immediate court date, there are some guidelines I recommend as I continue working with this Two-Home Family:

1. Both adults agree to stop the negative talk about one another to the boys.

2. Both adults are responsible for insuring their extended family members and/or friends do not bash the other parent.

3. Both adults agree to refrain from having overnight guest of the opposite sex when the boys are with them.

4. Both adults agree to address their own psychological issues and stop focusing on the other's character flaws. This would enable them to forgive and heal from the pain they have caused one another and it would free them to move forward in their parental roles.

5. Both adults agree to bring the children to therapy as directed and neither will coach or question that process.

6. Both adults will attend individual sessions where the objective will be to write a formal Parallel Co-Parenting Plan.

These are just some critical beginning stages for this family. It is imperative that the parents continue to see me in individual sessions while we develop a Parallel Co-Parenting Plan that will be submitted to the court.

Brenda Dozier, Ph.D., LMFT, LPC

Brenda Dozier, Ph.D.
Two-Home Family Therapy

118 N. Ross Street, Suite 6
PO Box 2056
Auburn, Alabama 36831
Phone: 334-821-3631
Fax: 334-821-3541
brendadozier@mindspring.com

March 9, 2003

Hon. John G. Doe
Two One Way Street
Honolulu, Alabama 36642

Re: Two-Home Family: Smith vs. Jones
Civil Action # DR-00-0000.0

Dear Judge Doe:

I have met with the above-referenced parents and their four children in six therapy sessions. Data from the sessions clearly indicates the children have suffered much pain as a consequence of the parental conflict following divorce.

Fortunately, the mother and father want to turn things around and therefore were willing to develop a cooperative co-parenting plan. This attached plan is child-centered and, if carried out in the daily lives of these Two-Home Family members, will reap benefits for all.

Thank you for sending this family system to me. I truly am grateful for your trust and confidence in my Two-Home Family model for preserving parent-child relationships.

If I can assist you any further on this case, please contact me.

Warm regards,

Brenda Dozier, Ph.D., LMFT, LPC
Two-Home Family Therapist
Xc: 2-Home Parents: James Jones, Suzy Smith; Attorneys: Billy Bob; Mary Kay
Attachment

Jones/Smith: Two-Home Family
March 9, 2003

The Jones/Smith Two-Home Family Cooperative Co-parenting Plan

1. We commit to being child-centered and doing what is in the best the best interest of our four beautiful children.

2. We recognize the importance of living in the same community and neither of us is planning to relocate.

3. We will not bash one another in front of our children.

4. We will reserve our "staff meetings" as the venue to discuss parenting unless an emergency requires otherwise. We agree to speak each Sunday evening at 6:30 for five to ten minutes over the telephone to review the upcoming week's parenting arrangements. If one of us gets upset or tries to discuss personal issues, we agree to hang up and try the talk two hours later.

5. We will both attend all sporting events and other activities our children participate in. When we see one another, we will be civil and will not do anything that would hurt or embarrass our children.

6. Because our earlier dating life was stressful to our children, we both agree to refrain from dating during the times the children are in our homes. From time to time, we will re-evaluate this issue and make changes as we believe the children are ready.

7. In both homes, we will make the children feel free and welcome to love, talk about the other parent, and display pictures of the other parent in their bedrooms and our family den.

8. We will pass along all information (report cards, schedules for baseball, karate, etc.) received during times the children are with us and will utilize the new mailboxes created with the children as the vehicle to do so.

9. We agree to report back to Two-Home Therapy if we have problems we are unable to resolve on our own.

_____   _____   _____
        Parent   Parent   Witness

References

Ahrons, Constance R. (1994). *The Good Divorce*. New York: HarperCollins.

Bohannon, Paul (1970). *Divorce and After.*

Dozier, Brenda. (2004). *For The Children's Sake: Parenting Together After the Marriage Ends.*

Dozier, B. S., Sollie, D. L., Stack, S. J., & Smith, T. A. (1993). Postdivorce Attachment and Coparenting Relationships, Journal of Divorce and Remarriage, 19, (3/4), 109-123. Reprinted in Everett, C. (Ed.) (1993). The Stepfamily Puzzle: Intergenerational Influences. New York: Haworth Press.

Gardner, Richard A. (1998). *The Parental Alienation Syndrome: A Guide for Mental Health and Legal Professionals* (2nd ed.). Creeskill, N.J.: Creative Therapeutics.

Goddard, W. K. & Dozier, B. S. (1995). *Parenting in Postdivorce Families*. Cooperative Extension Program Publication, Auburn University, Auburn, Alabama.

Statistical Abstract of the United States (2000). Washington, DC: U.S. Department of Commerce-Bureau of the Census.

Warshak, Richard A. (2001). *Divorce Poison. New York: ReganBooks.*

About the Author

Brenda Dozier, Ph.D., is a Licensed Marriage and Family Therapist, Clinical Member, Former Board Member, and Approved Supervisor of the American Association for Marriage and Family Therapy; a Licensed Professional Counselor and Counseling Supervisor for the Alabama Board of Examiners in Counseling; a part-time instructor at Troy State University, a mediator, and a national speaker. She is author of *For the Children's Sake: Parenting Together after the Marriage Ends*, a book for divorced parents. Dr. Dozier has also co-authored an article in the *Journal of Divorce and Remarriage* and an article in *Principles of Parenting* published by the extension service at Auburn University in Auburn, Alabama. She is founder and administrator of Auburn Family Therapy and lives in Auburn, Alabama.

0-595-31725-1

Printed in the United States
149525LV00002B/128/A

9 780595 317257